D1709357

Should We TRUST the News?

By Katie Kawa

KidHaven
PUBLISHING

Published in 2020 by
KidHaven Publishing, an Imprint of Greenhaven Publishing, LLC
353 3rd Avenue
Suite 255
New York, NY 10010

Designer: Deanna Paternostro
Editor: Katie Kawa

Photo credits: Cover wavebreakmedia/Shutterstock.com; p. 5 (top left) 0meer/
Shutterstock.com; p. 5 (top right) Kaspars Grinvalds/Shutterstock.com; p. 5 (bottom)
Rawpixel.com/Shutterstock.com; p. 7 George Rudy/Shutterstock.com; pp. 9, 13 (top) fizkes/
Shutterstock.com; p. 11 Ink Drop/Shutterstock.com; p. 13 (bottom) 1000 Words/Shutterstock.com;
p. 15 GaudiLab/Shutterstock.com; p. 17 JStone/Shutterstock.com; p. 19 George Sheldon/
Shutterstock.com; p. 21 (notepad) ESB Professional/Shutterstock.com; p. 21 (markers) Kucher
Serhii/Shutterstock.com; p. 21 (photo frame) FARBAI/iStock/Thinkstock; p. 21 (inset, left) MJTH/
Shutterstock.com; p. 21 (inset, middle) Syda Productions/Shutterstock.com; p. 21 (inset, right)
mavo/Shutterstock.com.

Cataloging-in-Publication Data

Names: Kawa, Katie.
Title: Should we trust the news? / Katie Kawa.
Description: New York : KidHaven Publishing, 2020. | Series: Points of view | Includes glossary and index.
Identifiers: ISBN 9781534529953 (pbk.) | ISBN 9781534567238 (library bound) | ISBN 9781534531208 (6 pack) | ISBN 9781534529960 (ebook)
Subjects: LCSH: Journalism–Objectivity–Juvenile literature. | Mass media–Objectivity–Juvenile literature.
Classification: LCC PN4784.O24 K39 2020 | DDC 302.23–dc23

Printed in the United States of America

CPSIA compliance information: Batch #BS19KL: For further information contact Greenhaven Publishing LLC, New York, New York at 1-844-317-7404.

Please visit our website, www.greenhavenpublishing.com. For a free color catalog of all our high-quality books, call toll free 1-844-317-7404 or fax 1-844-317-7405.

CONTENTS

A Matter of
TRUST

How do people learn about what's happening in the world around them? They often get this **information** by reading, watching, or listening to the news. There are many different news sources, or places where news comes from. Newspapers, TV news shows, websites, and **social media platforms** are some of the most popular news sources.

With so many news sources to choose from, it can be hard to know which ones to trust. People have different points of view about which news sources can be trusted to report the truth. These points of view **affect** how they get their news every day.

Know the Facts!

In a 2018 study, 69 percent of American adults said they trust the news less now than they did 10 years ago.

Should we trust the news? Some people believe the answer is always yes, some believe the answer is always no, and some believe it depends on the source of the news. Before you form your opinion on this issue, it's important to know all the facts!

The Need for
NEWS LITERACY

When people trust the news, they pay more attention to it, and this helps them become more informed, or educated, citizens. This was so important to the **Founding Fathers** that they made sure freedom of the press was included in the part of the U.S. **Constitution** called the Bill of Rights.

It's important to trust the news, but it's not always easy. Some sources that say they report the truth make up stories, and others share opinions instead of facts. However, people can learn to spot the differences between these sources and trustworthy ones.

Know the Facts!

A 2018 study showed that only 1 percent of Americans trust all news sources, and only 16 percent don't trust any news sources. Most Americans fall somewhere in between these two points of view.

News literacy is the ability to tell if a news source can be trusted. When people learn news literacy skills, they're more likely to trust the right news sources. They can also help other people learn how to find trustworthy news sources.

Fake
NEWS

News stories are supposed to be filled with facts, but sometimes people try to pretend **fiction** is news. These news stories, which are made up to purposely **mislead** people, are called fake news. In some cases, fake news stories have some facts in them to make them seem trustworthy, but most of the story is a lie.

Some websites have been created just to post fake news, and they often look like trustworthy websites. If people don't have news literacy skills, they can have a hard time spotting fake news, and they might share it by mistake.

Know the Facts!

In 2016, people from Russia spread fake news on social media because they believed it could affect how people voted in the U.S. presidential election. Other countries have also been affected by fake news from Russia.

Fake news is a major reason why people don't trust news sources. Some people believe it's safer not to trust any news than to trust a news story and then find out it was fake.

Is It Really FAKE?

Fake news is a big problem, and people around the world are working to fight it. However, some people claim fake news is more common than it actually is. This can make people even more confused about which news sources to trust.

Some powerful people use the words "fake news" to describe true news stories that they don't like or that make them look bad. These stories aren't really fake news. People who believe we should trust the news argue that it's harmful for powerful people to do this because many news sources can be trusted.

Know the Facts!

A major study of fake news in the United States was done in 2016. This study found that 84 percent of American adults believed they could spot a fake news story.

Many people have spoken out against the use of "fake news" to describe trustworthy news stories and sources. They believe it makes people less likely to trust news sources that are actually doing a good job of reporting the truth.

Sharing on
SOCIAL MEDIA

The internet is a major source of news for many people. Social media platforms allow people to share news quickly with a large audience. However, the news people share on social media isn't always true.

More than half of all people who get their news from social media expect it to be inaccurate, or incorrect. Many stories that are popular on social media are untrue or only partly true, but people often keep sharing them because they get attention. They sometimes do this even if they know a story isn't true.

Know the Facts!

As of late 2018, 68 percent of adults in the United States said they use social media for news. Most of the people who get their news from social media do so because they like how easy it is.

People at the center of a major event, such as a storm, a **protest**, or an act of **violence**, sometimes share their own reports about the event on social media. It's easy for someone who's not there to pretend they are and spread false information about what's happening.

Checking the
FACTS

Some people believe the internet makes it harder to trust the news, but other people believe it makes it easier. People can use the internet to help them spot fake news and find the true story. There are many trustworthy websites that can be used to check facts and sources from news shared on social media.

The internet allows people to find facts easier and faster than ever before. People who write news stories—often called journalists—can use these facts to make their stories as accurate as possible.

Know the Facts!

When American adults were asked what helped them decide to trust a news source, more than 70 percent said it was very important for the source to provide **links** to help them check the facts in the story online.

Journalists often use the internet to check the facts in their news stories. You can use the internet to check the facts too!

15

Being BIASED

Journalists are people, and people aren't perfect. They can make mistakes in their news stories, which sometimes makes it hard for people to trust what they're reporting. Also, journalists sometimes let their opinions and feelings affect how they report on an event or person.

Many people don't trust news sources that they believe are biased. A bias is an unfair belief that one person or thing is better than another. People often feel that news stories about **politics** are biased. In some cases, they won't trust a news source that doesn't share their opinions about the government.

Know the Facts!

A 2018 study about news sources and trust showed that bias is one of the main reasons why people don't trust the news. More than 40 percent of American adults said biased or unfair reporting was a reason they didn't trust certain news sources.

President Donald Trump has said that he feels some news sources write unfair stories about him. Many people agree with him, but others believe certain news sources are biased in his favor. Both groups of people believe the news isn't being reported fairly by certain journalists.

A Journalist's
JOB

Some news sources have clear biases, but in most cases, journalists don't let their feelings get in the way of their reporting. Most journalists studied how to report the news fairly and accurately in school, and they were trained to be trustworthy.

Professional journalists have rules they're supposed to follow, and one of the main rules is to "seek the truth and report it." If journalists do their job correctly, they keep their personal biases out of their stories and only report the facts. When people believe journalists are doing this, they're more likely to trust them.

Know the Facts!

Americans are more likely to trust local news than national news. In a 2018 study, more than 70 percent of Americans said they trusted local newspapers and TV news reports, but only around 50 percent of them trusted national or online news.

Most journalists believe they have a **responsibility**
to inform people about what's happening in the world
and to report the truth about important people and events.
They work hard to make sure people can trust them.

Not an Easy
QUESTION

Should we trust the news? After learning the facts, it's clear this isn't always an easy question to answer. Some websites, social media users, and other sources shouldn't be trusted. They post fake news and have clear biases. Other news sources, however, work hard to be trustworthy.

This is why news literacy is important. When people know which news sources to trust, they're more likely to be informed and active citizens. They're also more likely to use what they learn from the news to form their own educated opinions about the world around them.

Know the Facts!

In 2008, the News Literacy Project began working to teach news literacy in middle schools and high schools across the United States and around the world. Today, hundreds of thousands of students are learning news literacy skills because of this project.

Should we trust the news?

YES

- Some news stories that are called "fake news" are actually trustworthy.

- Journalists can use the internet to find facts to make their stories as accurate as possible.

- People can use the internet to check the facts in news stories and learn which sources to trust.

- Journalists are trained to be fair, to be accurate, and to report the truth.

NO

- Fake news is a big problem and makes it hard to know what sources to trust.

- Fake news gets spread quickly on social media because it gets a lot of attention.

- People can use social media to pretend they're reporting from a major event when they're not there.

- Journalists can make mistakes and sometimes have biases that affect their reporting.

These are some of the reasons people choose to either trust a news source or not trust one. It's important to treat each news story individually instead of deciding to trust or not trust all news sources.

GLOSSARY

affect: To produce an effect on something.

constitution: The basic laws by which a country, state, or group is governed.

fiction: A made-up story.

Founding Fathers: The leading figures in the founding of the United States.

information: Knowledge or facts about something.

link: A highlighted word or picture on a website that a person can click on to go to another website.

mislead: To cause someone to believe something that is not true.

politics: Activities and opinions that relate to the government.

professional: Having to do with a job someone does for a living.

protest: An event in which people gather to show they do not like something.

responsibility: A duty that a person should do.

social media platform: A website or application—also known as an app—that allows users to interact with each other and create online communities.

violence: The use of bodily force to hurt others.

For More
INFORMATION

WEBSITES

Get Smart About News

newslit.org/get-smart

This part of the News Literacy Project's website features quizzes and activities for kids and adults that test their news literacy skills.

"Spotting Fake News"

kids.nationalgeographic.com/explore/ngk-sneak-peek/april-2017/fake-news/

This article on the *National Geographic Kids* website features tips for finding fake news and links to videos and activities on this topic.

BOOKS

Dell, Pamela. *Understanding the News*. North Mankato, MN: Capstone Press, 2019.

Harris, Duchess. *Why News Matters*. Minneapolis, MN: Core Library, 2018.

Spanier, Kristine. *Facts and Opinions*. Minneapolis, MN: Pogo Books, 2019.

INDEX